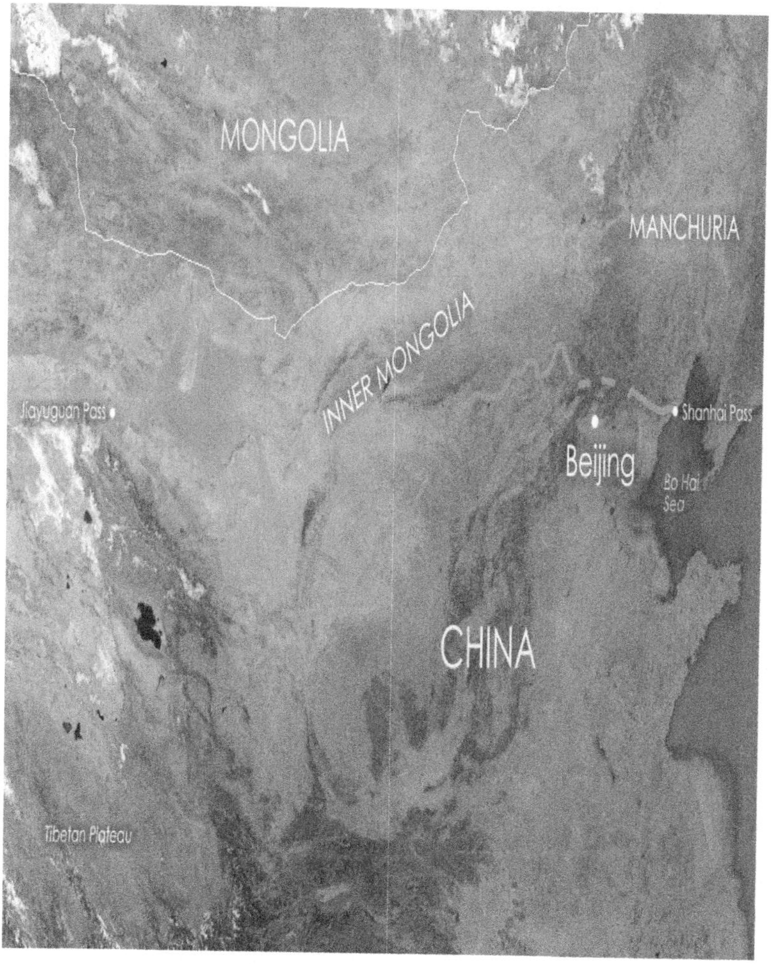
MONGOLIA
MANCHURIA
INNER MONGOLIA
Jiayuguan Pass
Shanhai Pass
Beijing
Bo Hai
Sea
CHINA
Tibetan Plateau

THE GREAT WALL OF CHINA TRAVEL GUIDE

WALKING THROUGH HISTORY: A JOURNEY ACROSS CHINA'S MOST ICONIC LANDMARK

AVERY WHITLOCK

All rights reserved.

No part of this publication may be reproduced, distributed, or transmitted in any form or by any means, including photocopying, recording, or other electronic or mechanical methods, without the prior written permission of the publisher, except in the case of brief quotations embodied in critical reviews and certain other noncommercial uses permitted by copyright law.

TABLE OF CONTENTS

1.0 INTRODUCTION TO THE GREAT WALL OF CHINA 6

1.1 A BRIEF HISTORY OF THE GREAT WALL 7

1.2 THE CULTURAL SIGNIFICANCE OF THE WALL 10

1.3 WHY VISIT THE GREAT WALL? 13

2.0 PLANNING YOUR TRIP TO THE GREAT WALL 19

2.1 BEST TIME TO VISIT 20

2.2 ENTRY FEES AND PERMITS 24

2.3 ESSENTIAL TRAVEL TIPS 27

3.0 THE MAIN SECTIONS OF THE GREAT WALL 36

3.1 BADALING: THE MOST POPULAR SECTION 38

3.2 MUTIANYU: A SCENIC AND LESS CROWDED SECTION 41

3.3 JIANKOU: THE WILD AND UNRESTORED WALL.......... 44

4.0 HIDDEN GEMS AND LESSER-KNOWN SECTIONS OF THE GREAT WALL.......... 51

4.1 JINSHANLING: THE PHOTOGRAPHER'S PARADISE.......... 52

4.2 SIMATAI: THE ONLY NIGHT-ACCESSIBLE SECTION.......... 55

4.3 GUBEIKOU: A SECTION FULL OF HISTORY.......... 58

5.0 HOW TO GET TO THE GREAT WALL....... 63

5.1 PUBLIC TRANSPORT OPTIONS.......... 64

5.2 PRIVATE TOURS AND GUIDED EXCURSIONS.......... 69

5.3 RENTING A CAR FOR A SELF-GUIDED TRIP.......... 74

6.0 HIKING THE GREAT WALL: WHAT YOU NEED TO KNOW.......... 80

6.1 BEST HIKING ROUTES FOR DIFFERENT SKILL LEVELS.......... 82

- 6.2 PACKING ESSENTIALS FOR A SAFE HIKE 88
- 6.3 SAFETY TIPS AND GUIDELINES 92

7.0 EXPERIENCING LOCAL CULTURE ALONG THE WALL 98

- 7.1 TRADITIONAL VILLAGES NEAR THE WALL 99
- 7.2 LOCAL CUISINE TO TRY 104
- 7.3 CULTURAL FESTIVALS AND EVENTS .111

8.0 PHOTOGRAPHY AND CAPTURING THE BEAUTY OF THE WALL 118

- 8.1 BEST SPOTS FOR STUNNING PHOTOS 120
- 8.2 PHOTOGRAPHY TIPS FOR DIFFERENT WEATHER CONDITIONS 127
- 8.3 USING DRONES: RULES AND REGULATIONS 132

9.0 ACCOMMODATION OPTIONS NEAR THE GREAT WALL 137

- 9.1 LUXURY HOTELS WITH A VIEW OF THE WALL.. 138
- 9.2 BUDGET-FRIENDLY GUESTHOUSES AND HOSTELS... 143
- 9.3 CAMPING ON THE GREAT WALL: IS IT ALLOWED?.. 148

10.0 UNIQUE WAYS TO EXPERIENCE THE GREAT WALL.. 155
- 10.1 GREAT WALL MARATHONS AND ADVENTURE ACTIVITIES........................... 156
- 10.2 CABLE CARS AND TOBOGGAN RIDES.... 160
- 10.3 HOT AIR BALLOON RIDES AND AERIAL VIEWS.. 163

11.0 THE FUTURE OF THE GREAT WALL: CONSERVATION AND PRESERVATION....... 168
- 11.1 CHALLENGES FACING THE WALL TODAY.. 169
- 11.2 RESTORATION EFFORTS AND HOW TO SUPPORT THEM.. 174

11.3 RESPONSIBLE TOURISM AND SUSTAINABLE TRAVEL.................................... 179

12.0 FINAL TRAVEL TIPS AND USEFUL RESOURCES....................................... 185

12.1 COMMON TOURIST MISTAKES TO AVOID.. 186

12.2 USEFUL PHRASES IN MANDARIN FOR TRAVELERS.. 191

12.3 RECOMMENDED TRAVEL APPS AND GUIDES... 195

CONCLUSION... 200

1.0 INTRODUCTION TO THE GREAT WALL OF CHINA

The Great Wall of China is one of the most extraordinary architectural wonders in the world. Stretching across vast landscapes, climbing rugged mountains, and winding through valleys, this ancient fortification is more than just a wall; it is a testament to human determination, ingenuity, and resilience. It has stood the test of time, bearing witness to centuries of history, battles, and the rise and fall of dynasties. Today, the Great Wall remains one of China's most visited landmarks, attracting millions of tourists from around the globe who come to marvel at its grandeur and immerse themselves in its historical significance.

1.1 A BRIEF HISTORY OF THE GREAT WALL

The origins of the Great Wall date back over 2,000 years to the Warring States period (475-221 BCE), when several feudal states in China built walls to defend their territories from invading nomadic tribes. However, it was during the Qin Dynasty (221-206 BCE) that Emperor Qin Shi Huang ordered the unification of these scattered walls into a single, continuous defense system.

This marked the beginning of what would later become one of the most formidable military structures in history.

During the Han Dynasty (206 BCE–220 CE), the wall was further extended to protect the Silk Road trade routes from hostile forces. The most famous and well-preserved sections of the wall, however, were constructed during the Ming Dynasty (1368–1644). Under the leadership of various Ming emperors, the wall was rebuilt and reinforced with bricks, stones, and watchtowers, transforming it into a stronghold against Mongol and other northern invasions.

Despite its immense scale and purpose, the Great Wall was never an impenetrable barrier. Instead, it functioned as a sophisticated defense network, incorporating beacons, signal towers, garrisons, and fortresses. Over the centuries, as China evolved and new military strategies emerged, the wall's defensive role diminished. Today, it stands as a powerful symbol of China's history, reflecting both the brilliance and the struggles of its past civilizations.

1.2 THE CULTURAL SIGNIFICANCE OF THE WALL

Beyond its military function, the Great Wall holds profound cultural significance for China and the world. It represents the perseverance and ambition of the Chinese people, embodying their ability to overcome challenges through unity and hard work.

The wall has been celebrated in Chinese literature,

poetry, and folklore for centuries, with countless stories depicting it as a guardian of the nation.

One of the most famous legends associated with the Great Wall is that of Meng Jiangnu, a woman whose husband was forced to work on the wall during the Qin Dynasty. When he perished due to the harsh labor, she is said to have wept so bitterly that a section of the wall collapsed, revealing his remains. This tale symbolizes both the immense human cost of building the wall and the deep emotional connection it has to the people of China.

The wall has also played a significant role in shaping China's national identity. It is often referred to as a defining feature of Chinese civilization, separating the agrarian culture of the central plains from the nomadic tribes of the north. In modern times, it has become a symbol of pride, resilience, and unity. The phrase "He who has never been to the Great Wall is not a true man" (不到长城非好汉), originally popularized by Mao Zedong, further emphasizes its importance in Chinese culture.

Today, the Great Wall is recognized as a UNESCO World Heritage Site and is celebrated as one of the New Seven Wonders of the World. It serves as a bridge between past and present, allowing visitors to connect with history while appreciating the sheer magnitude of human effort that went into its construction.

1.3 WHY VISIT THE GREAT WALL?

Visiting the Great Wall of China is a once-in-a-lifetime experience that offers breathtaking views, rich historical insights, and an unparalleled sense of adventure. There are countless reasons why travelers should make it a priority on their itinerary.

Firstly, the Great Wall offers an awe-inspiring visual spectacle. Whether standing atop its ancient ramparts or gazing at its winding path through mountains and valleys, visitors are treated to some of the most stunning landscapes in China. Each section of the wall provides a unique perspective, from the well-preserved Badaling section, which showcases the grandeur of Ming-era engineering, to the wild and rugged Jiankou section, which offers an adventurous hiking experience.

Beyond its beauty, the Great Wall provides a deep and immersive historical experience. Walking along its paths, visitors can imagine the thousands of soldiers who once stood guard, protecting the empire from invasions. The watchtowers and fortresses, still standing tall despite centuries of erosion, tell stories of fierce battles, strategic intelligence, and the sacrifices made by those who built and defended the wall.

Additionally, the Great Wall offers diverse activities for different types of travelers. Adventure seekers can take on the challenge of hiking along steep and unrestored sections, while history enthusiasts can explore museums and exhibits that provide deeper insights into its construction and significance.

Families can enjoy cable car rides to the top, while photographers will find endless opportunities to capture its magnificence from various angles.

Moreover, visiting the Great Wall allows travelers to connect with Chinese culture and traditions. Many sections of the wall are surrounded by ancient villages, traditional markets, and local restaurants where visitors can enjoy authentic Chinese cuisine. Some areas even offer cultural performances, reenacting historical battles and celebrating traditional Chinese customs.

Finally, the Great Wall is not just a relic of the past—it is a symbol of endurance, strength, and unity. Standing atop its ancient stones, feeling the weight of history beneath one's feet, is a humbling experience that reminds visitors of the power of human ambition and ingenuity. It is a place where history comes alive, offering a rare chance to walk in the footsteps of emperors, warriors, and builders who shaped China's legacy.

Whether you are drawn by its history, its breathtaking landscapes, or its cultural significance, the Great Wall of China promises an unforgettable journey.

It is more than just a travel destination—it is an experience that leaves a lasting impression, inspiring admiration for one of the greatest achievements in human history.

2.0 PLANNING YOUR TRIP TO THE GREAT WALL

Visiting the Great Wall of China is an exciting and unforgettable experience, but proper planning is essential to make the most of your journey. Given the vastness of the wall and the many different sections to explore, travelers need to consider the best time to visit, entry requirements, and key travel tips to ensure a smooth and enjoyable trip. From understanding the weather conditions to choosing the most suitable section of the wall, careful preparation will help you experience this world wonder to the fullest.

2.1 BEST TIME TO VISIT

The Great Wall can be visited year-round, but certain seasons offer better conditions for sightseeing and exploration. The best time to visit depends on weather preferences, crowd levels, and the type of experience you seek.

Spring (March to May) is one of the most popular times to visit. The weather is mild, with temperatures ranging between 10°C to 20°C (50°F to 68°F), making it perfect for hiking and sightseeing. The landscape comes alive with blooming flowers and lush greenery, providing a stunning backdrop for photography.

Summer (June to August) brings warmer temperatures, often reaching 30°C (86°F) or higher. While this is a great time for outdoor enthusiasts, it is also the peak tourist season, especially at well-known sections like Badaling and Mutianyu.

Expect large crowds and intense sunlight, so it's

important to bring plenty of water, wear sunscreen, and dress in lightweight, breathable clothing. The summer season also brings occasional rain showers, so carrying a light raincoat or umbrella is advisable.

Autumn (September to November) is arguably the best time to visit the Great Wall. The weather is cool and pleasant, with temperatures ranging from 10°C to 20°C (50°F to 68°F). The stunning fall foliage transforms the surrounding landscape into a breathtaking mix of red, orange, and gold hues, making it a favorite season for photographers and nature lovers. Tourist numbers begin to decline after China's National Day holiday in early October, allowing for a more relaxed and enjoyable visit.

Winter (December to February) offers a unique and serene experience of the Great Wall. With temperatures dropping below freezing, sections of the wall are often dusted with snow, creating a magical and peaceful atmosphere. This is the least crowded time to visit, making it perfect for those who prefer solitude and don't mind the cold. However, certain areas may be closed due to icy conditions, and visitors should dress in warm, layered clothing, wear non-slip shoes, and be prepared for strong winds.

2.2 ENTRY FEES AND PERMITS

The cost of visiting the Great Wall varies depending on the section you choose to explore. Each section is managed separately and has its own entry fees, which may also include optional services like cable car rides, shuttle buses, and chair lifts. Below are some of the most visited sections along with their general admission costs:

- **Badaling**: One of the most popular and well-preserved sections, Badaling charges an entry fee of approximately 40-45 RMB (around $6-$7 USD) during peak season. A round-trip cable car ticket costs around 140 RMB ($20 USD).
- **Mutianyu**: Known for its scenic beauty and fewer crowds, Mutianyu's entrance fee is around 40 RMB ($6 USD), with optional cable car rides costing an additional 120-140 RMB ($17-$20 USD).
- **Jinshanling**: This section is favored by hikers for its mix of restored and wild areas. Entry costs about 65 RMB ($9 USD).
- **Simatai**: The only section open for night tours, Simatai's entrance fee is around 40

RMB ($6 USD), with night tickets costing around 80 RMB ($11 USD).

- **Jiankou**: This is a rugged, unrestored section that requires no official entry fee, but it is more challenging to reach and hike.

For most visitors, a standard entry ticket is sufficient, but if you plan to hike or camp overnight in certain sections, additional permits may be required. It's always advisable to check the latest fees and regulations before your trip, as prices and policies can change.

2.3 ESSENTIAL TRAVEL TIPS

A trip to the Great Wall is a rewarding experience, but preparation is key to ensuring a smooth and enjoyable visit. Here are some essential travel tips to consider:

1. **Choose the Right Section**

    The Great Wall is vast, and each section offers a unique experience. Badaling and Mutianyu are the most tourist-friendly, with well-preserved paths and amenities, making them ideal for first-time visitors and families. Those seeking adventure can explore Jinshanling or Jiankou, which offer steep climbs and wilder landscapes. Simatai is perfect for those interested in experiencing the Wall at night.

2. **Arrive Early to Avoid Crowds**

Popular sections like Badaling can get extremely crowded, especially on weekends and during Chinese holidays. Arriving early in the morning, ideally before 9 AM, will help you beat the rush and enjoy a quieter experience.

3. **Wear Comfortable Footwear**

The Great Wall is known for its steep and uneven steps, so wearing sturdy, comfortable walking shoes or hiking boots is essential. Avoid sandals or flip-flops, as they offer little support on the rugged terrain.

4. **Bring Plenty of Water and Snacks**

   While some sections have small vendors selling drinks and snacks, prices can be high, and options may be limited. Carrying your own water and lightweight snacks, such as energy bars or fruit, will keep you refreshed during your hike.

5. **Dress in Layers and Prepare for Weather Changes**

   The weather on the Great Wall can change quickly, especially in mountainous areas. Dressing in layers allows you to adjust to temperature fluctuations. In summer, wear a hat and sunscreen to protect against the sun, while in winter, gloves and a warm jacket are essential.

6. **Respect the Wall and Its History**

 The Great Wall is a UNESCO World Heritage Site and an important part of China's history. Avoid littering, graffiti, or damaging any part of the structure. Some sections have signs prohibiting climbing on certain parts of the wall—respect these rules to help preserve the site for future generations.

7. **Be Prepared for Physical Challenges**

Walking the Great Wall can be physically demanding, with steep inclines, uneven steps, and long distances. Take breaks when needed, pace yourself, and listen to your body.

8. **Consider Hiring a Guide**

   A knowledgeable guide can provide historical insights and interesting facts that enhance your experience. Many sections of the Wall offer guided tours in multiple languages.

9. **Check Transportation Options in Advance**

   Most sections of the Wall are located outside Beijing, and transportation can vary. While Badaling is accessible by train and bus, other sections like Mutianyu require private transport or organized tours. Knowing your transportation options beforehand will save time and hassle.

10. Capture the Moment

The Great Wall is one of the most photogenic landmarks in the world. Bring a good camera or smartphone to capture the stunning landscapes. For the best shots, explore less crowded areas and take photos during sunrise or sunset for dramatic lighting.

Visiting the Great Wall of China is an experience that leaves a lasting impression. With proper planning, the right timing, and a little preparation, your journey to this historic wonder will be unforgettable. Whether you choose to explore its most famous sections or venture into its wild and untouched areas, the Great Wall offers a glimpse into China's rich past and an adventure like no other.

3.0 THE MAIN SECTIONS OF THE GREAT WALL

The Great Wall of China stretches across thousands of miles, winding through rugged mountains, deserts, and valleys. Due to its immense length, it is divided into several sections, each with its own unique characteristics, history, and accessibility. Some parts of the wall have been restored and are well-preserved for tourists, while others remain in their wild, unrestored state, offering an adventurous experience.

Choosing the right section to visit depends on your preferences—whether you seek an easy and family-friendly walk, a scenic escape from the crowds, or a challenging hike along crumbling ancient stones. Among the numerous sections, three stand out as the most significant and frequently visited: Badaling, Mutianyu, and Jiankou. Each provides a distinct perspective on the Great Wall, allowing visitors to explore it in different ways.

3.1 BADALING: THE MOST POPULAR SECTION

Badaling is the most famous and heavily visited section of the Great Wall. Located about 70 kilometers (43 miles) northwest of Beijing, it is the best-preserved and most accessible section, making it a top choice for first-time visitors. Built during the Ming Dynasty (1368–1644), Badaling was strategically significant as a military stronghold protecting Beijing from invasions. Today, it continues to serve as a symbol of China's rich history and cultural heritage.

One of the main reasons for Badaling's popularity is its accessibility. It is the only section of the Great Wall connected to Beijing via direct train and bus routes, making it the easiest to reach. The section is also equipped with modern facilities, including visitor centers, souvenir shops, restaurants, and cable cars, allowing people of all ages and fitness levels to experience the wall.

Walking along Badaling, visitors will find wide, well-maintained pathways and sturdy stone steps, making it comfortable to explore.

However, this convenience also means that Badaling is often crowded, especially during weekends and holidays. If you prefer a peaceful experience, it's best to visit early in the morning or on weekdays.

Despite the large crowds, Badaling offers breathtaking panoramic views of the surrounding mountains, making it a fantastic place for photography. The sheer size and grandeur of the wall here give visitors a true appreciation of the scale of this ancient structure.

3.2 MUTIANYU: A SCENIC AND LESS CROWDED SECTION

Mutianyu is another well-preserved section of the Great Wall, known for its beautiful scenery, fewer crowds, and family-friendly atmosphere. Located about 73 kilometers (45 miles) northeast of Beijing, Mutianyu is an excellent alternative to Badaling for those who want a more relaxed and scenic experience.

This section of the wall dates back to the Northern Qi Dynasty (550–577 AD) but was later reinforced during the Ming Dynasty. It features 23 watchtowers, offering spectacular views of rolling hills covered in lush greenery during spring and summer, vibrant autumn foliage, and a snow-covered wonderland in winter.

One of the highlights of Mutianyu is its balance between restoration and authenticity. While the pathways are well-maintained, much of the original structure remains intact, allowing visitors to see the ancient craftsmanship of the wall. The stone bricks, arched gateways, and watchtowers create an immersive historical experience.

Mutianyu also offers several options for reaching the top. Visitors can hike up the stone steps for a rewarding climb, take a cable car for a more relaxed journey, or ride a toboggan down for a fun and unique descent. These features make it a great choice for families and casual travelers who want to experience the Great Wall without the overwhelming crowds of Badaling.

Although Mutianyu is slightly harder to reach than Badaling, it is still accessible via bus, taxi, or private tour. Its combination of stunning landscapes, rich history, and peaceful atmosphere makes it one of the best sections for those looking to truly appreciate the beauty of the Great Wall.

3.3 JIANKOU: THE WILD AND UNRESTORED WALL

For adventure seekers and experienced hikers, Jiankou offers the most thrilling and challenging experience on the Great Wall.

Located about 100 kilometers (62 miles) from Beijing, Jiankou is a completely unrestored section, known for its steep, crumbling paths, dramatic cliffs, and rugged beauty. Unlike the well-maintained Badaling and Mutianyu sections, Jiankou has been left in its natural state, making it both dangerous and awe-inspiring.

Jiankou was built during the Ming Dynasty and features some of the most striking architecture of the Great Wall. The watchtowers here stand tall against jagged mountain peaks, and the wall itself follows the sharp ridges of the mountains, creating breathtaking and intimidating views. The most famous part of Jiankou is the "Sky Stairway," a near-vertical climb that challenges even the most experienced hikers.

Due to its dangerous terrain, Jiankou is not officially open for tourists, and visiting requires careful preparation. Unlike Badaling and Mutianyu, there are no cable cars, handrails, or safety barriers, meaning visitors must be in excellent physical condition and fully aware of the risks. Many sections of the wall here are partially collapsed, with loose bricks and steep drops, making it essential to wear proper hiking gear and bring plenty of water and supplies.

Despite these challenges, those who brave Jiankou are rewarded with an unparalleled experience. The lack of crowds allows for a peaceful and intimate connection with history, and the raw, untamed beauty of the landscape makes it one of the most photogenic sections of the Great Wall.

Jiankou is especially popular among photographers who seek dramatic sunrise and sunset shots over the untouched ruins.

For those who want to experience Jiankou but prefer a safer route, a popular option is to hike from Jiankou to Mutianyu. This allows visitors to enjoy the rugged, wild section before transitioning into the more restored and tourist-friendly part of the wall.

In conclusion, the Great Wall of China is not just one continuous structure but a series of distinct sections, each offering a unique experience. Whether you prefer the convenience and grandeur of Badaling, the scenic charm of Mutianyu, or the wild and adventurous terrain of Jiankou, there is a section suited to every type of traveler.

Badaling remains the top choice for first-time visitors due to its accessibility and well-preserved paths, while Mutianyu provides a quieter and more scenic alternative with modern amenities. Meanwhile, Jiankou challenges the boldest adventurers with its dramatic landscapes and raw history.

No matter which section you choose to visit, standing atop the Great Wall, gazing out over the vast mountains and ancient stonework, is an experience that leaves a lasting impression. The Great Wall of China is not only a symbol of China's past but also a testament to human resilience, determination, and architectural brilliance.

4.0 HIDDEN GEMS AND LESSER-KNOWN SECTIONS OF THE GREAT WALL

While sections like Badaling and Mutianyu are the most visited and well-maintained, the Great Wall of China stretches far beyond these popular areas. For travelers seeking a more authentic, less crowded, and visually stunning experience, the lesser-known sections of the Wall offer breathtaking landscapes, rich history, and unique adventures. Among these hidden gems, **Jinshanling, Simatai, and Gubeikou** stand out as extraordinary destinations for those looking to explore the Wall beyond the tourist-heavy spots.

4.1 JINSHANLING: THE PHOTOGRAPHER'S PARADISE

Nestled between Simatai and Gubeikou, **Jinshanling** is regarded as one of the most picturesque sections of the Great Wall. Its combination of **original ruins and restored areas** provides a perfect setting for photography enthusiasts, offering dramatic landscapes, crumbling watchtowers, and long, winding paths that disappear into the horizon.

One of the defining features of Jinshanling is its **architectural diversity.** The Wall here showcases different styles of construction, including **varied watchtower designs, sharp inclines, and strategically built fortifications.** Unlike the smooth, fully restored paths of Badaling, Jinshanling offers an authentic mix of well-preserved sections and partially eroded walls, giving visitors a true sense of the Wall's age and endurance.

Another reason Jinshanling is a favorite for photographers is its **stunning sunrise and sunset views**. Since this section is less crowded, early morning and late evening hikes allow for an **uninterrupted experience of golden hues spreading over the mountains**, making it a dream location for capturing the Wall's majestic beauty.

For visitors who love hiking but prefer a **moderate challenge**, Jinshanling is an ideal choice. The hike is not as physically demanding as Jiankou, yet it still offers an **adventurous experience** with varying terrain, steep ascents, and panoramic views that stretch for miles.

4.2 SIMATAI: THE ONLY NIGHT-ACCESSIBLE SECTION

For those seeking a **one-of-a-kind experience**, Simatai is the only section of the Great Wall that remains **open for night visits**.

Located about 120 km from Beijing, this section offers a unique opportunity to see the Wall illuminated under the stars, creating an **atmosphere of mystery and grandeur**.

Simatai is known for its **steep and rugged terrain**, with some sections nearly vertical. It is one of the most well-preserved original sections, with features dating back to the Ming Dynasty. Walking along its pathways, visitors can see ancient **bricks still**

bearing the marks of their original craftsmen, giving an authentic glimpse into history.

For those who prefer not to hike, Simatai offers a **cable car ride** that takes visitors up the Wall, providing **breathtaking aerial views of the surrounding valleys and lakes**. The nearby **Gubei Water Town** is another highlight, offering a chance to explore traditional Chinese architecture, cultural performances, and even hot springs—making it an excellent option for a more immersive historical and relaxing experience.

At night, **soft golden lighting** transforms Simatai into an enchanting sight, with the glowing Wall snaking through the dark mountains, creating a view unlike any other. Whether you choose to hike at dusk, take a cable car ride under the moonlight, or simply gaze at the Wall from a nearby vantage point, Simatai promises an **unforgettable adventure.**

4.3 GUBEIKOU: A SECTION FULL OF HISTORY

For history buffs, **Gubeikou** is one of the most significant and least restored sections of the Great Wall.

Unlike the more tourist-friendly areas, Gubeikou retains its **wild, rugged, and battle-scarred appearance**, providing a raw and authentic glimpse into the past.

This section has seen **numerous battles throughout Chinese history**, serving as a key military stronghold due to its strategic location. Visitors can still see **bullet holes and damage from**

past conflicts, making it one of the most historically rich parts of the Wall. Walking along Gubeikou, one can almost **feel the echoes of ancient warriors and defenders who once guarded China's borders.**

One of the **biggest attractions** of Gubeikou is its **tranquility**. Since it is far less crowded than places like Badaling or Mutianyu, visitors can explore the Wall **without the usual tourist rush**, making it perfect for those who want to appreciate the historical and natural beauty of the site in peace.

Hiking at Gubeikou is a **true adventure**, as many parts of the Wall here are **crumbling, uneven, and overgrown with vegetation**. Unlike the well-maintained sections, Gubeikou's paths remain mostly untouched, offering a **sense of raw exploration**. However, due to its remote nature, it is advisable to **travel with a guide or in a group**, as some areas are not clearly marked and can be challenging to navigate.

For travelers who wish to explore beyond the crowded and commercialized sections of the Great Wall, **Jinshanling, Simatai, and Gubeikou** offer truly unique experiences. Whether you are looking for **stunning photography spots, a rare chance to explore the Wall at night, or a deep dive into history,** these lesser-known sections provide a more intimate and rewarding adventure.

Each of these locations presents its own challenges and highlights, but they all share one thing in common—**an awe-inspiring view of one of the world's greatest wonders.** If you are planning a trip to the Great Wall and want to go beyond the usual tourist spots, consider venturing into these hidden gems for an unforgettable journey.

5.0 HOW TO GET TO THE GREAT WALL

Reaching the Great Wall of China is an essential part of planning your visit, as its immense length means there are multiple entry points spread across different regions. The best way to get to the Wall depends on which section you want to visit, your budget, and how much time you have.

For travelers coming from Beijing, the most accessible sections are Badaling, Mutianyu, Jinshanling, Jiankou, and Simatai. Each of these sections offers a different experience, from well-preserved and tourist-friendly areas to rugged and remote hiking trails. You can choose between public transport, private tours, or renting a car, each offering distinct advantages depending on your preferences.

5.1 PUBLIC TRANSPORT OPTIONS

For budget-conscious travelers or those who enjoy independent exploration, public transportation is the most affordable way to get to the Great Wall.

While it may take longer than a private car or tour, it offers an authentic travel experience and the opportunity to see more of the local surroundings.

1. **Bus to Badaling:**

    Badaling is the easiest section to reach using public transport. The most convenient way is taking the **S2 train from Huangtudian Railway Station** in Beijing to Badaling Railway Station. The train ride takes about 1.5 hours. Alternatively, you can take **Bus 877 from Deshengmen** in central Beijing, which is a direct and affordable option. The journey takes about 1.5 to 2 hours.

2. **Bus to Mutianyu:**

Mutianyu is not directly accessible by train, but you can take **Bus 916 Express** from Dongzhimen Public Transport Hub in Beijing to Huairou, then transfer to a local bus or taxi to reach Mutianyu. This journey takes around 2 to 2.5 hours in total. Another option is taking the **Mutianyu Direct Bus**, which departs from Dongzhimen and takes about 1.5 hours.

3. **Bus to Jinshanling and Simatai:**

These sections are further away, requiring more travel time. You can take a long-distance bus from **Beijing Dongzhimen or Wangjing West Station** to

Luanping, then transfer to a local shuttle or taxi to reach the entrance. Travel time is around 3 to 4 hours, making these sections better suited for an overnight stay or a full-day excursion.

4. **Trains to the Great Wall:**

   The **high-speed train from Beijing North Railway Station to Badaling Great Wall Station** is the fastest public transport option, taking around 40 minutes. However, train access to other sections like Mutianyu or Jiankou is not available, so you'll need to rely on buses or private transport.

While public transportation is economical, it requires careful planning, as some buses run on limited schedules. It's also best to check the latest routes and timetables in advance, as changes can occur.

5.2 PRIVATE TOURS AND GUIDED EXCURSIONS

For those who prefer a hassle-free experience, **private tours and guided excursions** are a great option. These tours typically include round-trip transportation, an English-speaking guide, entrance fees, and sometimes meals, ensuring a smooth and informative visit.

1. **Group Tours:**

    Many travel agencies in Beijing offer **group tours to Badaling and Mutianyu**, which are the most popular sections. These tours are ideal for travelers who want a cost-effective and structured itinerary. Group tours typically include hotel pick-up and drop-off, making transportation convenient. However, they may have a fixed schedule and less flexibility.

2. **Private Tours:**

Private guided tours offer more **personalized experiences**, allowing you to explore the Wall at your own pace. A professional guide can provide in-depth historical insights, making your visit more engaging and meaningful. Private tours are particularly beneficial if you plan to visit remote sections like Jiankou or Simatai, as they include customized routes and transport arrangements.

3. **Hiking and Photography Tours:**

For adventure seekers, there are specialized **hiking and photography tours** that focus on the wilder, less-visited sections of the Wall. These tours are great for those who want to capture stunning sunrise or sunset views, explore unrestored ruins, or trek across

76

multiple sections in one day.

4. **Night Tours at Simatai:**

   Simatai is one of the only sections of the Great Wall open for night visits. Some private tours offer guided night hikes, providing a unique opportunity to see the Wall illuminated under the stars. This experience is perfect for those seeking a magical and less crowded atmosphere.

Private tours are more expensive than public transport, but they offer comfort, convenience, and a deeper understanding of the history and significance of the Wall.

5.3 RENTING A CAR FOR A SELF-GUIDED TRIP

For travelers who value freedom and flexibility, **renting a car** is an excellent way to visit the Great Wall at your own pace. Driving allows you to explore multiple sections in a single trip and avoid the limitations of public transport schedules.

1. **Renting a Car in Beijing:**

    Many international and local car rental agencies operate in Beijing, offering both self-drive and chauffeur services. If you don't have a **Chinese driver's license**, you'll need to hire a local driver, as **foreign licenses are not valid in China** without a temporary permit. Hiring a driver ensures a smooth journey without worrying about navigation or traffic rules.

2. **Recommended Driving Routes:**

    ○ **Beijing to Badaling:** Approximately **1.5 hours (70 km/43 miles)** via the **G6 Expressway.**

- Beijing to Mutianyu: Around **1.5 to 2 hours (73 km/45 miles)** via the **G101 Highway.**
- Beijing to Jinshanling or Simatai: Roughly **2.5 to 3 hours (150 km/93 miles)** via the **G45 Expressway.**

3. **Advantages of Driving:**

    - You can **avoid crowded buses and tour groups**.
    - You have the freedom to **explore at your own pace** and visit multiple sections in a single day.
    - You can bring more **travel gear, snacks, and photography equipment** without worrying about luggage restrictions.

4. **Challenges of Driving:**

    - **Heavy traffic in Beijing** can make driving stressful, especially during peak hours.

- **Parking availability** at some Great Wall sections may be limited, requiring early arrival.
- **Navigating rural roads** to remote sections can be difficult without GPS or Chinese-language maps.

Getting to the Great Wall of China depends on your travel style, budget, and preferred level of convenience. **Public transportation is the most economical choice**, but it requires time and careful planning. **Private tours offer a stress-free experience** with expert guidance, making them ideal for first-time visitors. **Renting a car provides the most freedom**, but it requires familiarity with China's road regulations.

Regardless of how you get there, visiting the Great Wall is a once-in-a-lifetime experience. Whether you choose a scenic drive, a historical tour, or an adventurous hike, the journey to this world-famous landmark is as rewarding as the destination itself.

6.0 HIKING THE GREAT WALL: WHAT YOU NEED TO KNOW

Hiking the Great Wall of China is one of the most exhilarating and rewarding experiences for any traveler. Stretching over 13,000 miles, the Wall traverses rugged mountains, lush valleys, and remote desert landscapes. Whether you're an experienced trekker or a casual visitor looking for a scenic walk, the Great Wall offers a variety of hiking experiences suited for all levels.

Unlike a simple visit to one of the tourist-friendly sections, hiking the Wall provides a deeper appreciation of its grandeur, history, and the sheer effort it took to construct. However, hiking the Wall requires preparation, as some sections are steep, unrestored, and physically demanding. This guide will help you choose the best hiking routes, prepare essential gear, and ensure your safety along the way.

6.1 BEST HIKING ROUTES FOR DIFFERENT SKILL LEVELS

The Great Wall consists of multiple sections, some of which are well-preserved, while others are rugged and untouched. Depending on your fitness level, time constraints, and preference for scenery or solitude, you can choose from the following routes:

Beginner-Friendly Hikes (Easy to Moderate)

1. **Badaling Section** – This is the most famous and well-restored part of the Great Wall, located about 70 km from Beijing. It is an excellent choice for first-time visitors or those looking for a relaxed walk with stunning views. The pathways are wide, and cable cars are available for those who prefer to avoid steep climbs.

2. **Mutianyu Section** – Slightly less crowded than Badaling, Mutianyu offers a scenic and moderate hike. It has restored watchtowers

and a smoother walking surface. There is also a cable car and a fun toboggan ride for descending, making it suitable for families and casual hikers.

3. **Huanghuacheng Section** – Known as the "Water Great Wall," this section features part of the Wall submerged in a lake. It offers a unique hiking experience with moderate difficulty and beautiful views. It's

an excellent option for those looking for a less touristy area while still enjoying a comfortable hike.

Intermediate Hikes (Moderate to Challenging)

4. **Jinshanling to Simatai** – This 10 km hike is one of the most popular routes for adventurous travelers. It offers a mix of restored and wild Wall sections, providing a balance of history and challenge. The hike takes about 4-5 hours and includes steep climbs and breathtaking scenery.

5. **Gubeikou Section** – A less-visited but historically significant part of the Wall,

Gubeikou retains much of its original structure. The hike is moderately challenging with uneven terrain, but it offers incredible views and a sense of authenticity. It is ideal for those who want to explore a quieter, less-commercialized part of the Wall.

Advanced Hikes (Challenging and Remote)

6. **Jiankou Section** – Considered the most dangerous and challenging part of the Great Wall, Jiankou is an unrestored section with steep cliffs, broken pathways, and crumbling towers. It is recommended for experienced hikers who are comfortable with rock scrambling and have proper hiking gear. The reward is an unparalleled view of the Wall winding through rugged mountain peaks.

7. **Shanhaiguan (Old Dragon's Head) to Jiaoshan** – This unique hike starts at the easternmost point of the Great Wall, where it meets the Bohai Sea. The terrain is steep, with long climbs and breathtaking coastal views. It's an ideal trek for those who want

to experience both the Wall and the sea.

Each of these hikes offers a different perspective on the Great Wall, from its architectural grandeur to its wild and untouched beauty. It's important to choose a route that matches your fitness level and interest to ensure an enjoyable experience.

6.2 PACKING ESSENTIALS FOR A SAFE HIKE

Hiking the Great Wall requires proper preparation, especially if you're venturing into remote or challenging sections. Here are the essential items to bring for a safe and comfortable hike:

Clothing and Footwear

- Wear **comfortable, moisture-wicking clothing** suitable for the season. In summer, lightweight clothing with sun protection is essential, while in winter, layers and a windproof jacket are necessary.
- **Hiking boots or sturdy shoes** with good grip are essential for handling uneven terrain, especially on unrestored sections.

Food and Water

- Carry **at least 2 liters of water per person**, as there are few places to refill, especially on remote hikes.
- Bring **energy snacks** like nuts, dried fruit, protein bars, or sandwiches to keep your energy levels up during long hikes.

Safety and Navigation

- A **map or GPS device** is useful, especially in lesser-known sections where signage is limited.
- A **fully charged phone** with a power bank in case of emergencies. While some sections have mobile coverage, remote parts may not.

- A **first-aid kit** with bandages, antiseptic wipes, pain relievers, and any personal medications.
- **Sunscreen, sunglasses, and a hat** to protect against strong sun exposure.

Additional Essentials

- **A small backpack** to carry your belongings comfortably.
- **A lightweight rain jacket or poncho** if hiking in the rainy season.
- **Hiking poles** for added stability on steep or rugged sections.
- **A flashlight or headlamp** if planning a sunset or sunrise hike.

By packing wisely, you can ensure a comfortable and safe hiking experience, whether you're on a short walk or a multi-hour trek.

6.3 SAFETY TIPS AND GUIDELINES

The Great Wall, especially in its wild and unrestored sections, can be physically demanding and unpredictable. Following these safety guidelines will help you avoid potential hazards:

1. **Know Your Limits** – Choose a section that matches your fitness level. Some parts of the Wall have extreme inclines and crumbling pathways that can be dangerous for inexperienced hikers.

2. **Check the Weather Forecast** – The weather can change quickly, especially in mountainous areas. Avoid hiking in extreme heat, heavy rain, or during winter snowstorms. Wet surfaces can be slippery,

and fog can obscure visibility.

3. **Start Early** – Many sections of the Wall have long, challenging trails that take several hours to complete. Starting early ensures you have enough daylight to finish your hike safely.

4. **Stay on Marked Paths** – Some sections have steep drop-offs and loose stones. Stick to established trails and avoid walking on edges or climbing unstable structures.

5. **Beware of Wildlife and Insects** – In remote sections, you may encounter wild animals or insects like ticks and mosquitoes. Wearing

long sleeves and using insect repellent can help prevent bites.

6. **Respect the Heritage** – The Great Wall is a UNESCO World Heritage Site. Avoid vandalizing, littering, or taking bricks as souvenirs. Preserve the Wall for future generations.

7. **Inform Someone About Your Plans** - If hiking alone or in remote areas, let someone know your itinerary and expected return time. In case of an emergency, this information can be crucial.

8. **Use a Guide for Unfamiliar Routes** - If you're unfamiliar with a section, hiring a local guide can enhance your experience and help you navigate safely. Guides can provide historical context and ensure you don't get lost.

Hiking the Great Wall is an unforgettable adventure that allows you to experience its breathtaking landscapes and historical legacy.

Whether you're taking a leisurely stroll along a well-preserved section or trekking through rugged, untamed parts of the Wall, preparation and safety should always be a priority.

With the right planning, gear, and mindset, your journey along this ancient wonder will be a memorable and awe-inspiring experience.

7.0 EXPERIENCING LOCAL CULTURE ALONG THE WALL

Visiting the Great Wall of China is not just about witnessing an architectural wonder; it's also an opportunity to immerse yourself in the rich cultural heritage that surrounds this ancient structure. Beyond the breathtaking views and historical significance, the regions near the Wall are home to vibrant traditions, charming villages, and unique culinary delights. Travelers who take the time to explore the local culture will gain a deeper appreciation of the Wall's enduring legacy and the people who have lived in its shadow for centuries.

From picturesque villages that have preserved their ancient ways of life to mouthwatering regional cuisine and lively festivals, experiencing the local culture along the Great Wall transforms your trip into a truly unforgettable journey.

7.1 TRADITIONAL VILLAGES NEAR THE WALL

Scattered along the length of the Great Wall, numerous villages have stood for centuries, their histories intertwined with the Wall itself. These villages offer a glimpse into traditional Chinese rural life, allowing visitors to step back in time and experience the customs, architecture, and hospitality of the local people.

1. **Gubeikou Village** – Located near the Gubeikou section of the Wall, this village retains its old-world charm with well-preserved courtyard homes,

stone-paved streets, and a laid-back atmosphere. It is an excellent place to interact with local farmers, hear stories about the Wall, and enjoy peaceful countryside scenery.

2. **Huanghuacheng Village** – This village is famous for its proximity to the "Water Great Wall," where part of the Wall is submerged in a reservoir. Here, visitors can stay in family-run guesthouses, enjoy fresh farm-to-table meals, and hike through lush landscapes. The village is particularly beautiful in summer when yellow

wildflowers bloom across the hills.

3. **Mutianyu Village** – Situated near the popular Mutianyu section, this village blends tradition with modern convenience. It features rustic guesthouses, handicraft shops, and local eateries where visitors can sample home-cooked meals. The village is

also a great base for those looking to explore the Wall at a relaxed pace.

4. **Shuiguan Village** – Close to the Badaling and Juyongguan sections, this small village offers a quieter alternative to the heavily touristed areas nearby. It provides an authentic glimpse into the lives of the locals who have lived near the Wall for generations.

5. **Cuandixia Village** – While not directly beside the Great Wall, Cuandixia is a well-preserved Ming Dynasty village worth visiting. Located about 90 km from Beijing, it is home to ancient stone houses, narrow alleys, and stunning mountain scenery. It is an excellent side trip for those interested in traditional Chinese architecture and history.

Visiting these villages offers a rare opportunity to experience China beyond its modern cities, where traditions are still alive, and the Wall is not just a tourist attraction but a part of daily life.

7.2 LOCAL CUISINE TO TRY

One of the highlights of exploring the Great Wall region is indulging in the local cuisine, which reflects the flavors of northern China. Whether you are dining in a small village restaurant, a family-run guesthouse, or a bustling street market, you will find delicious and hearty dishes that have been enjoyed for centuries.

1. **Beijing Roast Duck (Peking Duck)** – While famous in Beijing, this dish is also popular in villages near the Wall. The crispy, succulent duck is served with thin pancakes, scallions, cucumber, and sweet bean sauce.

2. **Zha Jiang Mian (Fried Sauce Noodles)** – A traditional northern Chinese noodle dish made with thick wheat noodles topped with a savory-sweet soybean paste sauce, minced pork, and fresh vegetables. It is a simple yet flavorful meal enjoyed by locals and travelers alike.

3. **You Po Mian (Hand-Pulled Oil Noodles)** – A specialty of northern China, these thick,

chewy noodles are tossed with hot oil, garlic, chili, and soy sauce, creating a fragrant and spicy dish.

4. **Mongolian Hot Pot** – In areas closer to Inner Mongolia, such as Gubeikou, hot pot is a popular dish, especially in winter. Diners cook thinly sliced lamb, vegetables, and

noodles in a steaming pot of flavorful broth.

5. **Shaobing (Sesame Flatbread)** – A crispy, flaky bread often stuffed with fillings such as minced pork, scallions, or red bean paste. It is a great snack to take on a hike along the Wall.

6. **Dumplings (Jiaozi)** – A staple in northern China, dumplings are filled with minced pork, beef, or vegetables and are either boiled, steamed, or pan-fried. They are often served with vinegar and chili sauce.

7. **Donkey Burger (Lü Rou Huo Shao)** – A unique specialty in the region, this dish consists of shredded donkey meat stuffed in a crispy, layered bun. It may sound unusual, but it is a local delicacy with a rich and savory taste.

8. **Tofu Dishes** – Villages near the Wall often serve homemade tofu dishes, including stir-fried tofu with vegetables or spicy mapo

tofu, a Sichuan-style dish with a bold and fiery flavor.

Many guesthouses and village restaurants offer farm-to-table meals using fresh, local ingredients. Dining in these traditional settings allows travelers to taste authentic northern Chinese flavors while enjoying warm hospitality.

7.3 CULTURAL FESTIVALS AND EVENTS

Throughout the year, various cultural festivals and events take place in the Great Wall region, celebrating history, heritage, and local traditions. Attending one of these festivals adds an extra layer of excitement to your visit.

1. **Chinese New Year (Spring Festival)** – Celebrated nationwide, Chinese New Year brings festive decorations, temple fairs, and traditional performances to villages near the Wall. Fireworks, dragon dances, and family feasts are common highlights.

2. **Great Wall Marathon** – Held annually in May, this marathon is one of the most challenging races in the world, with participants running along steep sections of the Wall at Jinshanling and Simatai. Even if you're not competing, it's an exciting event to witness.

3. **Mid-Autumn Festival** – Also known as the Moon Festival, this event takes place in September or October. Locals gather to enjoy mooncakes, light lanterns, and admire the full moon. The festival is a magical time to visit the Wall, as many celebrations include music and storytelling.

4. **Dragon Boat Festival** – This traditional festival, held in June, commemorates the ancient poet Qu Yuan. Villages near the Wall may host dragon boat races in nearby rivers, along with traditional food like zongzi (sticky rice dumplings wrapped in bamboo leaves).

5. **Temple Fairs** – Some villages host temple fairs during special occasions, where visitors can experience folk performances, acrobatics, and traditional handicrafts. These fairs are a great way to see local artisans at work and buy unique souvenirs.

6. **Lantern Festival** – Marking the end of Chinese New Year celebrations, the Lantern Festival sees streets and temples adorned with colorful lanterns. Visitors can enjoy traditional snacks, solve lantern riddles, and watch lion and dragon dances.

Attending these festivals provides an enriching cultural experience, allowing travelers to connect with local traditions and witness the lively spirit of the communities near the Great Wall.

Experiencing the local culture along the Great Wall adds depth and meaning to your journey. While the Wall itself is a historical marvel, the people, traditions, and culinary delights that surround it make for an unforgettable adventure. Whether you are wandering through ancient villages, savoring local delicacies, or taking part in a cultural festival, immersing yourself in the rich heritage of the region will leave you with a deeper appreciation for this iconic wonder of the world.

8.0 PHOTOGRAPHY AND CAPTURING THE BEAUTY OF THE WALL

The Great Wall of China is one of the most photogenic landmarks in the world. Spanning rugged mountains, dense forests, and sweeping plains, its sheer length and historical significance make it a dream destination for photographers. Whether you are a professional with high-end equipment or a traveler with just a smartphone, capturing the Wall's grandeur requires careful planning, an eye for detail, and an understanding of the best locations and conditions.

Photography at the Great Wall presents unique opportunities but also some challenges. Different sections of the Wall offer distinct landscapes, lighting conditions vary throughout the day, and weather can greatly affect your shots. Knowing where to go and how to prepare can help you take breathtaking photographs that do justice to this world-famous wonder.

8.1 BEST SPOTS FOR STUNNING PHOTOS

The Great Wall stretches over 21,000 kilometers, but some sections are particularly well-suited for capturing its beauty. Whether you're looking for dramatic landscapes, historic ruins, or scenic perspectives, these locations provide incredible photography opportunities.

1. **Badaling – Iconic and Classic Views**

   Badaling is the most famous and well-preserved section, offering classic postcard-style shots of the Wall winding across the mountains. The advantage of this location is its accessibility and restored condition, making it ideal for clear, high-resolution images. However, because of its popularity, it is best to visit early in the morning or on weekdays to avoid large crowds.

2. **Mutianyu – Stunning Scenery and Fewer Tourists**

   Known for its well-restored walls and lush surroundings, Mutianyu provides spectacular photo opportunities with fewer visitors compared to Badaling.

3. The cable car and toboggan ride add unique elements for storytelling through your photographs. The panoramic views from the watchtowers at Mutianyu are especially breathtaking.

4. **Jinshanling – The Photographer's Favorite**

   This section is a paradise for photographers. Jinshanling features a mix of restored and wild Wall, allowing you to capture both history and nature in one frame. The rolling hills, crumbling watchtowers, and golden sunlight at sunrise or sunset make it one of the most photogenic sections of the Wall. It's less crowded, offering uninterrupted shots.

5. **Jiankou – The Wild and Dramatic Wall**

   If you're looking for adventure and raw beauty, Jiankou is the perfect place. This unrestored section features steep inclines, overgrown vegetation, and crumbling stonework, giving it an authentic and rugged appearance. The "Sky Stairway" and "Eagle Flying Over the Wall" are particularly dramatic photography spots, but reaching them requires a challenging hike.

6. **Huanghuacheng – The Wall by the Water**

One of the most unique sections, Huanghuacheng is partially submerged in a reservoir, creating beautiful reflections on the water. During summer, the hills are covered in yellow wildflowers, adding vibrant color to your shots. The contrast between the Wall and the serene lake makes for a truly breathtaking image.

7. **Gubeikou – Historical and Less Touristy**

    This section is rich in history and relatively untouched by restoration efforts, giving it a raw and ancient feel. The views here are expansive, and since it is not as frequented by tourists, you can take uninterrupted shots of the Wall stretching endlessly across the hills.

8. **Simatai – Nighttime Photography Opportunities**

Simatai is the only section of the Wall open for night tours, offering an entirely different photography experience. The illuminated Wall against the dark sky creates a mystical atmosphere, perfect for capturing dramatic nighttime shots. The reflections of the lights in the nearby water town also provide great compositions.

8.2 PHOTOGRAPHY TIPS FOR DIFFERENT WEATHER CONDITIONS

Weather conditions at the Great Wall can vary greatly depending on the season and time of day. Being prepared for different lighting and atmospheric conditions will help you capture stunning images.

1. **Sunny Days – High Contrast and Vivid Colors**

    - Use a polarizing filter to reduce glare and enhance the blue sky.
    - Shoot early in the morning or late in the afternoon for softer light and fewer shadows.

- If photographing at midday, adjust your exposure settings to avoid overly bright highlights.

2. **Cloudy or Overcast Days – Soft and Even Lighting**

    - Overcast skies can create a moody and dramatic effect, ideal for emphasizing the Wall's texture.
    - Increase the contrast in post-processing to add depth to your images.
    - Use the mist or fog to your advantage, capturing a mystical and mysterious look.

3. **Winter – Snow-Covered Beauty**

- The Great Wall covered in snow is breathtaking but requires careful exposure adjustments to avoid overexposure.
- Wear gloves that allow you to operate your camera easily, as temperatures can be extremely cold.

- Capture footprints in the snow for a storytelling element in your composition.

4. **Spring – Vibrant Colors and Blooming Flowers**

    - Cherry blossoms and wildflowers near the Wall add beautiful pops of color to your shots.
    - Use a wide aperture to create a shallow depth of field, making the flowers stand out against the Wall.

5. **Summer – Greenery and Bright Light**

- Expect hazy conditions due to humidity; use a lens hood to reduce glare.
- Capture reflections in lakes or rivers near the Wall, such as at Huanghuacheng.
- Drink plenty of water and protect your camera from heat damage.

6. **Autumn – Golden and Red Hues**

    - Fall is one of the best seasons for photography, with the foliage turning shades of red, orange, and gold.
    - Experiment with different angles to incorporate colorful leaves in the foreground.

- Use a tripod for sharp landscape shots, especially in lower light conditions.

8.3 USING DRONES: RULES AND REGULATIONS

Drones provide an incredible way to capture aerial views of the Great Wall, but strict regulations must be followed. China has specific laws regarding drone usage, and not all areas of the Wall allow drone flights.

1. **Where Can You Fly a Drone?**
    - Some remote sections like Jinshanling and Jiankou are more lenient with drone usage.
    - Areas such as Badaling and Mutianyu have strict no-fly zones due to their status as major tourist attractions.
2. **Regulations to Keep in Mind**
    - A permit may be required for commercial drone photography.
    - Drones should not be flown near large crowds or sensitive areas.

- The maximum altitude allowed by Chinese aviation law is 120 meters (394 feet).

3. **Tips for Drone Photography**

    - Plan your flight path in advance to avoid restricted areas.

- Check the weather conditions, as strong winds can make drone operation difficult.
- Capture wide-angle shots to highlight the scale of the Wall against the surrounding landscape.
- Always carry extra batteries, as cold weather can drain them faster.

Photography at the Great Wall is an unforgettable experience that allows you to capture the beauty, history, and grandeur of this legendary structure. By choosing the right locations, adjusting to different weather conditions, and following regulations for drone usage, you can create stunning images that reflect the true essence of the Wall. Whether you're shooting dramatic landscapes, timeless portraits, or intricate architectural details, every photo you take will be a testament to the enduring legacy of one of the world's greatest wonders.

9.0 ACCOMMODATION OPTIONS NEAR THE GREAT WALL

Visiting the Great Wall of China is a once-in-a-lifetime experience, and choosing the right accommodation can enhance your trip significantly. Whether you are looking for a luxury hotel with breathtaking views, a budget-friendly guesthouse close to a hiking trail, or an adventurous camping experience, there are plenty of options near different sections of the Wall.

The type of accommodation you choose depends on your itinerary, preferred level of comfort, and how close you want to stay to the Wall itself. While many visitors choose to stay in Beijing and take a day trip, staying overnight near the Wall allows you to experience the site in a more peaceful and immersive way, especially during sunrise and sunset when the crowds are minimal.

9.1 LUXURY HOTELS WITH A VIEW OF THE WALL

For travelers who want to enjoy the Great Wall in comfort and style, there are a few high-end hotels that offer stunning views and premium services. These accommodations provide an unforgettable experience with top-notch hospitality, fine dining, and direct access to some of the most scenic sections of the Wall.

1. **Commune by the Great Wall** (near Badaling and Shuiguan)

   This luxury resort is one of the most famous high-end accommodations near the Wall. The hotel consists of a collection of designer villas built into the surrounding landscape, offering a private and exclusive stay. Some rooms have floor-to-ceiling windows that provide breathtaking views of the Wall from your bed. The resort also offers private hiking trails to secluded sections of the Wall.

2. **Brickyard Retreat at Mutianyu**

   Located close to the Mutianyu section, this eco-friendly retreat is a perfect choice for those who want a balance of luxury and nature. It is set in a restored tile factory and features comfortable rooms with large windows overlooking the Wall. The hotel offers a peaceful atmosphere, organic farm-to-table meals, and spa treatments to relax after a long day of hiking.

3. **Dhawa Jinshanling**

This upscale hotel near Jinshanling provides a tranquil and stylish stay for visitors who want to explore the less crowded and picturesque parts of the Wall. It combines modern comfort with a traditional Chinese aesthetic, and many rooms offer direct views of the Wall in the distance.

4. **Gubei Water Town Hotels (near Simatai)**

    Gubei Water Town is a reconstructed ancient-style town located at the foot of the Simatai section. Several boutique hotels and resorts within the town offer elegant accommodations with a mix of modern and traditional Chinese decor. Staying here gives you a unique opportunity to explore Simatai at night, as it is the only section open after sunset.

9.2 BUDGET-FRIENDLY GUESTHOUSES AND HOSTELS

For travelers who prefer budget-friendly options, there are many local guesthouses, hostels, and homestays near different sections of the Wall.

These accommodations offer a more authentic experience, as they are often run by local families who provide home-cooked meals and cultural insights.

1. **Great Wall Box House (Gubeikou)**

    This small and cozy guesthouse is located near the wild and unrestored section of Gubeikou. It is a great option for budget travelers who want to stay in a traditional Chinese courtyard home. The friendly hosts can arrange guided hikes to Gubeikou,

Jinshanling, and even Jiankou.

2. **Yardstay at Mutianyu**

A charming countryside guesthouse close to Mutianyu, Yardstay offers clean and simple rooms with a rustic atmosphere. The owners are known for their hospitality and can help arrange transportation to the Wall. It's an excellent choice for those who want a quiet, family-run place to stay.

3. **Happy Lodge (Huanghuacheng)**

This budget-friendly lodge near Huanghuacheng is a favorite among hikers. The rooms are basic but comfortable, and the guesthouse provides delicious homemade meals. It is located close to the scenic reservoir section of the Wall, making it a perfect spot for nature lovers.

4. **Simatai Great Wall Youth Hostel**

Located within Gubei Water Town, this hostel offers affordable dormitory-style and private rooms with easy access to the Simatai Wall. The atmosphere is lively, making it a great place for backpackers to meet fellow travelers.

5. **Camping-Style Guesthouses in Jiankou**

    Since Jiankou is a wild and unrestored section, there are no large hotels nearby. However, small local guesthouses offer a place to rest before and after your hike.

    These accommodations are very basic, often

with shared bathrooms, but they provide an authentic rural experience.

9.3 CAMPING ON THE GREAT WALL: IS IT ALLOWED?

Camping on the Great Wall is a dream for many adventure travelers, offering the chance to experience the site in its most peaceful and undisturbed state. However, the legality of camping depends on the section of the Wall you visit.

Where Is Camping Allowed?

1. **Jiankou** – This wild and unrestored section is one of the most popular places for camping, as there are no official regulations

strictly prohibiting it. Many hikers pitch tents inside old watchtowers for shelter. However, it is important to be mindful of safety, as the terrain can be steep and unstable.

2. **Gubeikou** – Another good spot for camping, as it is less regulated than the more touristy sections. Many local guides offer overnight

hiking tours with camping included.

3. **Huanghuacheng** – Some parts of this section allow camping, especially in the more remote areas. The combination of the Wall and the nearby reservoir makes for an incredibly scenic overnight stay.

Where Is Camping Prohibited?

- **Badaling, Mutianyu, and Simatai** – These sections are strictly monitored and do not allow camping due to their status as major tourist attractions. Rangers patrol these areas to prevent overnight stays.
- **Jinshanling** – Camping is officially not allowed, but some local guides offer overnight stays just outside the Wall.

Tips for Camping on the Great Wall

- **Pack light but bring essential gear** – A lightweight tent, sleeping bag, and warm clothing are necessary, as temperatures drop at night.

- **Bring enough food and water** – There are no facilities on the wild sections, so you must carry all necessary supplies.
- **Be mindful of the environment** – Leave no trace by carrying out all trash and avoiding damage to the Wall.
- **Check the weather before camping** – Rain can make the stone surfaces slippery, and strong winds can be dangerous at high altitudes.

- **Consider hiring a guide** – If you're unfamiliar with the area, having a local guide can help you navigate safely.

Finding the right accommodation near the Great Wall can significantly enhance your travel experience. Luxury travelers can enjoy breathtaking views and world-class services, while budget-conscious travelers can find affordable guesthouses with warm hospitality. For the most adventurous visitors, camping on the Wall offers an unforgettable experience, but it requires careful planning and adherence to local regulations.

No matter where you choose to stay, waking up near one of the greatest architectural wonders in history is an experience that will stay with you forever.

10.0 UNIQUE WAYS TO EXPERIENCE THE GREAT WALL

The Great Wall of China is one of the most awe-inspiring historical sites in the world, stretching thousands of kilometers across rugged terrain. While most visitors experience the Wall through traditional sightseeing or hiking, there are several unique and adventurous ways to make your visit truly unforgettable. From marathons and adventure sports to aerial views and exhilarating toboggan rides, there are numerous ways to explore this legendary structure beyond just walking along its ancient stones.

10.1 GREAT WALL MARATHONS AND ADVENTURE ACTIVITIES

For those seeking a more physically challenging way to experience the Great Wall, participating in a marathon or an adventure activity is an incredible option. These activities combine endurance, history, and breathtaking scenery, making for an unforgettable experience.

Great Wall Marathons

One of the most famous and demanding marathons in the world, the **Great Wall Marathon** is held annually at the Huangyaguan section of the Wall. This challenging race includes steep ascents, thousands of stone steps, and rugged mountain paths, testing even the most experienced runners. Participants can choose between a full marathon (42 km), a half marathon (21 km), and a fun run (8.5

km), each offering spectacular views of the surrounding countryside.

Running on the Wall is not just about endurance; it is also about experiencing history in a way that few others do. As you pass through ancient watchtowers and climb steep staircases, you'll be reminded of the immense effort that went into building this massive structure centuries ago.

Rock Climbing and Rappelling

For adventure enthusiasts, sections of the Wall near Jiankou and Simatai offer opportunities for rock climbing and rappelling. Jiankou, known for its wild and unrestored appearance, has steep cliffs and challenging rock formations that attract climbers looking for a thrilling experience.

Rappelling down sections of the Wall provides a unique perspective and an adrenaline rush unlike any other.

Cycling Along the Wall

While cycling on the Wall itself is not permitted, several routes run parallel to the structure, particularly near the **Gubeikou and Huanghuacheng** sections. These paths take cyclists through stunning landscapes, offering both a challenging and rewarding way to experience the Wall from a different angle. Some guided tours include biking along scenic countryside trails, stopping at various access points along the Wall.

10.2 CABLE CARS AND TOBOGGAN RIDES

For visitors who prefer a more relaxed and scenic way to explore the Wall, cable cars and toboggan rides provide a unique alternative to climbing the steep stone steps. These options allow visitors of all ages and fitness levels to enjoy the beauty of the Wall without the physical strain of hiking.

Cable Cars: A Comfortable Ride to the Top

Many of the most visited sections of the Great Wall, including **Mutianyu, Badaling, and Simatai**, offer cable cars that transport visitors to the higher points of the Wall.

These rides provide a spectacular aerial perspective

as they glide over the forested mountains, revealing breathtaking views of the ancient structure winding through the landscape.

The **Mutianyu Cable Car** takes visitors up to a high watchtower, allowing easy access to some of the most scenic parts of the Wall. Similarly, the **Badaling Cable Car** makes this popular section more accessible, especially for elderly visitors or those with mobility challenges.

Toboggan Rides: A Thrilling Descent

One of the most fun and unexpected ways to descend the Great Wall is via the **Mutianyu Toboggan Ride**. This exhilarating slide takes visitors down a winding metal track from the Wall back to the entrance area. The ride lasts several minutes and allows you to control your speed with a simple lever, making it an exciting yet safe activity for visitors of all ages.

The toboggan ride is particularly popular among families with children and adventurous travelers who want to add an element of fun to their visit. It's a refreshing way to descend after a long hike, replacing the usual steep staircases with a fast and thrilling ride through the mountains.

10.3 HOT AIR BALLOON RIDES AND AERIAL VIEWS

For a once-in-a-lifetime experience, seeing the Great Wall from the air offers a breathtaking perspective that few visitors get to enjoy.

The vastness of the Wall, stretching endlessly over mountains and valleys, becomes even more impressive when viewed from above.

Hot Air Balloon Rides

At certain locations, such as **Gubeikou and Jinshanling**, hot air balloon tours provide a truly magical way to witness the Wall's grandeur. These rides typically take place early in the morning or late in the afternoon, when the soft golden light enhances the beauty of the surrounding landscape.

Floating silently above the Wall, you'll get an unparalleled view of its winding path through the rugged mountains, surrounded by lush forests, farmlands, and historic villages. This peaceful yet exhilarating experience is perfect for couples, photographers, or anyone looking for a unique way to appreciate the scale and beauty of the Great Wall.

Helicopter Tours

For those who prefer a faster-paced aerial experience, **helicopter tours** over the Great Wall offer a thrilling way to take in its magnificence. These tours operate mainly over the **Badaling and**

Mutianyu sections and provide a bird's-eye view of the Wall as it snakes over the dramatic terrain.

Helicopter rides are ideal for travelers who want a luxurious and exclusive way to see the Wall, as well as for photographers looking to capture breathtaking panoramic shots. The tours typically last between 10 to 30 minutes, offering ample time to admire and photograph the Wall from above.

Experiencing the Great Wall of China goes beyond just walking along its ancient paths. Whether you're pushing your physical limits in a marathon, soaring above the Wall in a hot air balloon, or gliding down a thrilling toboggan ride, there are countless ways to make your visit truly unforgettable.

For those seeking adventure, rock climbing, cycling, and extreme sports provide a heart-pounding way to connect with the Wall's rugged landscape. If you prefer a more relaxed experience, cable cars and helicopter tours offer stunning views without the physical exertion. No matter which unique experience you choose, visiting the Great Wall is bound to be one of the most memorable journeys of a lifetime.

11.0 THE FUTURE OF THE GREAT WALL: CONSERVATION AND PRESERVATION

The Great Wall of China, an architectural marvel spanning over 21,000 kilometers, has withstood the test of time for centuries. However, despite its grandeur and historical significance, the Wall faces numerous challenges that threaten its integrity and longevity. From natural erosion to human interference, preserving this UNESCO World Heritage Site requires extensive efforts and global cooperation. Conservation and restoration projects are in place, but sustainable tourism and responsible travel play crucial roles in ensuring that future generations can continue to experience the magnificence of this ancient wonder.

11.1 CHALLENGES FACING THE WALL TODAY

The Great Wall's existence is at risk due to various factors, including environmental conditions, human activities, and economic development. While certain sections of the Wall, such as Badaling and Mutianyu, are well-preserved and maintained, other remote and unrestored areas are crumbling, with some sections disappearing entirely.

Natural Erosion and Climate Change

One of the biggest threats to the Great Wall is **natural erosion**. Over centuries, exposure to wind, rain, and extreme temperature changes has caused severe deterioration. The Wall's **earthen sections**, particularly in desert areas such as Gansu and Inner Mongolia, are highly vulnerable to wind erosion, while sections built with brick and stone suffer from water damage and freeze-thaw cycles that weaken their structure.

With the effects of **climate change**, the Wall faces increasing risks. Rising temperatures and changing weather patterns accelerate erosion, while heavy rainfall and floods have led to collapses in certain areas. Stronger storms and unpredictable natural disasters continue to pose a threat to its stability.

Vandalism and Unregulated Tourism

Human activities have also played a significant role in damaging the Great Wall. In some areas, **tourists carve graffiti into the bricks**, steal stones as souvenirs, or leave litter behind. Unregulated tourism has led to increased foot traffic in fragile areas, causing wear and tear on the already weakened structures.

Some sections of the Wall have been commercialized to accommodate tourists, leading to **overcrowding and excessive development**. The Badaling section, for example, receives millions of visitors annually, putting strain on its pathways, watchtowers, and surrounding infrastructure.

Urbanization and Illegal Construction

Urban expansion and infrastructure development have also contributed to the destruction of parts of the Wall. In the past, **local residents used bricks from the Wall for construction**, unknowingly causing irreversible damage. Even today, **illegal construction projects and road developments** near the Wall threaten its surroundings, further compromising its preservation.

11.2 RESTORATION EFFORTS AND HOW TO SUPPORT THEM

Recognizing the importance of preserving this cultural treasure, the Chinese government and international organizations have launched numerous restoration and conservation projects. However, striking a balance between preservation and authenticity remains a challenge, as some restoration efforts have been criticized for using modern materials that do not match the original construction.

Government Initiatives

The **State Administration of Cultural Heritage** in China has implemented laws and regulations to protect the Great Wall. Restoration projects have been carried out at key sites such as **Mutianyu, Jinshanling, and Simatai**, where expert craftsmen use traditional techniques to restore damaged sections while maintaining historical accuracy.

Additionally, in 2016, the **Great Wall Protection Plan** was introduced, aiming to regulate tourism, prevent illegal activities, and increase monitoring of endangered sections. The use of **modern**

technology, such as drones and satellite imaging, has also helped experts track the Wall's condition and detect early signs of structural damage.

Community and Volunteer Programs

Many **non-governmental organizations (NGOs) and volunteer groups** have joined conservation efforts, focusing on restoring lesser-known and neglected sections of the Wall. Some of these programs allow tourists and history enthusiasts to participate in **brick-laying activities, educational workshops, and cleanup campaigns.**

Organizations such as the **China Great Wall Society** and the **International Friends of the Great Wall** work to raise awareness and funds for conservation projects. Supporting these initiatives, either through donations or volunteering, can contribute significantly to the preservation of the Wall.

How You Can Help

Visitors to the Great Wall can play an active role in its conservation by following **responsible tourism practices**:

- **Do not deface or remove any part of the Wall.** Avoid carving names, drawing graffiti, or taking bricks as souvenirs.
- **Stay on designated paths.** Walking off-trail can accelerate erosion and damage fragile areas.
- **Dispose of waste properly.** Leaving litter behind harms both the environment and the Wall's historical integrity.
- **Support ethical tourism businesses.** Choose tour operators and local guides who promote sustainable travel and respect preservation rules.
- **Educate others.** Raising awareness about the importance of conservation helps ensure long-term protection efforts.

11.3 RESPONSIBLE TOURISM AND SUSTAINABLE TRAVEL

Sustainable tourism is key to preserving the Great Wall while allowing future generations to continue enjoying its splendor. Travelers must be mindful of their impact and adopt responsible behaviors when visiting historical sites.

Choosing Less Crowded Sections

One way to reduce overcrowding and lessen the environmental impact is by **visiting less popular sections** of the Wall. While Badaling remains the most visited, other sections like **Huanghuacheng, Gubeikou, and Jiankou** offer a more peaceful experience while helping to distribute foot traffic more evenly across the Wall.

Eco-Friendly Practices

Adopting **eco-friendly travel habits** can contribute to the sustainability of the Great Wall:

- **Use reusable water bottles** instead of single-use plastics.
- **Choose eco-friendly accommodations** that follow sustainable practices.
- **Respect local wildlife and vegetation** by not picking plants or disturbing animals near the Wall.

Supporting Local Communities

Many villages near the Wall rely on tourism for economic survival. Instead of opting for large commercial chains, consider staying in **locally owned guesthouses,** eating at **family-run**

restaurants, and purchasing handmade souvenirs from artisans.

This supports local businesses and encourages sustainable economic development.

The Great Wall of China stands as a symbol of resilience, strength, and history, but its future depends on conscious efforts to protect and preserve it. Natural erosion, vandalism, and urbanization pose significant challenges, but with government initiatives, community involvement, and responsible tourism, we can ensure that this ancient wonder remains intact for generations to come.

By making thoughtful travel choices, respecting preservation rules, and supporting conservation projects, every visitor can contribute to the Wall's legacy.

The Great Wall is not just a relic of the past—it is a living testament to human ingenuity, and its survival depends on how we choose to protect it today.

12.0 FINAL TRAVEL TIPS AND USEFUL RESOURCES

A journey to the Great Wall of China is a once-in-a-lifetime experience, offering breathtaking views, deep historical insights, and an adventure unlike any other. However, proper planning is essential to make the most of your visit. From avoiding common mistakes to learning useful phrases in Mandarin and utilizing helpful travel apps, being well-prepared will ensure a smooth and enjoyable trip. This final section provides essential travel tips and resources to help you navigate the Wall with confidence and ease.

12.1 COMMON TOURIST MISTAKES TO AVOID

Even the most seasoned travelers can make mistakes when visiting the Great Wall. Learning from others' experiences can help you avoid unnecessary hassles and make the most of your adventure. Here are some common pitfalls and how to avoid them:

1. Visiting Only the Most Touristy Sections

Many tourists head straight to the Badaling

section, which is the most accessible but also the most crowded. While it offers well-preserved architecture and easy transportation, the experience can feel rushed and overly commercialized.

If you prefer a more immersive experience, consider exploring sections like Jinshanling, Simatai, or

Gubeikou, which offer stunning scenery and fewer crowds.

2. Underestimating the Physical Challenge

Hiking the Great Wall is not a simple walk in the park. Many sections have steep inclines, uneven steps, and long stretches of rugged terrain. Some visitors arrive unprepared, wearing inappropriate footwear or lacking water. Make sure to wear **comfortable hiking shoes**, carry **plenty of water**, and dress appropriately for the weather.

3. Not Checking the Weather Forecast

Weather conditions can significantly impact your experience. The Wall can be extremely cold and windy in winter, scorching hot in summer, and slippery after rain. Always check the forecast before your trip and dress in layers to adapt to sudden changes in temperature.

4. Ignoring Local Regulations and Etiquette

Climbing on unauthorized sections of the Wall, leaving litter, or carving names into the bricks are all actions that harm the site and show disrespect. Be mindful of conservation efforts and adhere to signs and guidelines. Responsible tourism ensures that the Wall is preserved for future generations.

5. Arriving Without Enough Cash

While larger sections of the Wall accept credit cards, smaller and more remote areas often do not. Some local food vendors, entrance fees, and transportation options require **cash payments**. It's advisable to carry **Chinese yuan (RMB)** in small denominations to cover unexpected expenses.

6. Not Planning for Transportation

Many visitors assume they can simply take a taxi to the Wall and easily return. However, some sections, especially the more remote ones, do not have frequent return transportation. If you're not part of a guided tour, make sure to arrange **round-trip transport** or confirm your return options before setting out.

12.2 USEFUL PHRASES IN MANDARIN FOR TRAVELERS

While major tourist sections of the Wall have English signage and some English-speaking staff, venturing into less commercialized areas may require some basic Mandarin. Learning a few essential phrases can make communication much easier.

Basic Greetings and Politeness:

你好 (Nǐ hǎo) – Hello

谢谢 (Xièxiè) – Thank you

请 (Qǐng) – Please

对不起 (Duìbùqǐ) – Sorry

再见 (Zàijiàn) – Goodbye

Asking for Directions:

请问, 长城在哪里? (Qǐngwèn, Chángchéng zài nǎlǐ?) - Excuse me, where is the Great Wall?

我怎么去长城? (Wǒ zěnme qù Chángchéng?) - How do I get to the Great Wall?

这个方向对吗? (Zhège fāngxiàng duì ma?) - Is this the right direction?

At Restaurants and Shops:

这个多少钱? (Zhège duōshǎo qián?) - How much is this?

我要这个 (Wǒ yào zhège) - I want this one

有没有英文菜单? (Yǒu méiyǒu yīngwén càidān?) - Do you have an English menu?

Emergencies and Help:

帮帮我! (Bāng bāng wǒ!) – Help me!

我迷路了 (Wǒ mílù le) – I'm lost

我需要医生 (Wǒ xūyào yīshēng) – I need a doctor

If you're not confident in speaking Mandarin, downloading a **translation app** such as Google Translate can help with real-time communication.

12.3 RECOMMENDED TRAVEL APPS AND GUIDES

In today's digital age, having the right travel apps can make navigating the Great Wall and its surrounding areas much easier. Here are some must-have apps to enhance your trip:

1. Baidu Maps (百度地图)

Google Maps does not work reliably in China due to internet restrictions. Instead, Baidu Maps is the go-to navigation app for finding your way around cities and rural areas. While primarily in Chinese, it is highly accurate and can be used with **automatic translation tools.**

2. WeChat (微信)

WeChat is China's most widely used messaging

and payment app. It is helpful for **contacting local tour guides, booking transportation, and even making mobile payments** at many stores and restaurants.

3. Didi (滴滴出行)

Didi is China's version of Uber and is an essential app for booking rides, especially if you're traveling outside Beijing and need to reach more remote sections of the Wall. Some drivers understand basic English, but it's useful to have your destination written in Chinese.

4. Google Translate or Pleco

For quick translations, **Google Translate** works well for both text and voice input. However, since internet restrictions in China may block some Google services, **Pleco** is a great offline Mandarin-English dictionary that does not require an internet connection.

5. Ctrip (携程) or Trip.com

This app helps with booking hotels, train tickets, and guided tours. It offers English-language support and is widely used by travelers in China.

6. China Train Booking App

If you plan to take a train to reach Beijing before heading to the Great Wall, this app is extremely helpful for **checking train schedules and booking tickets in advance.**

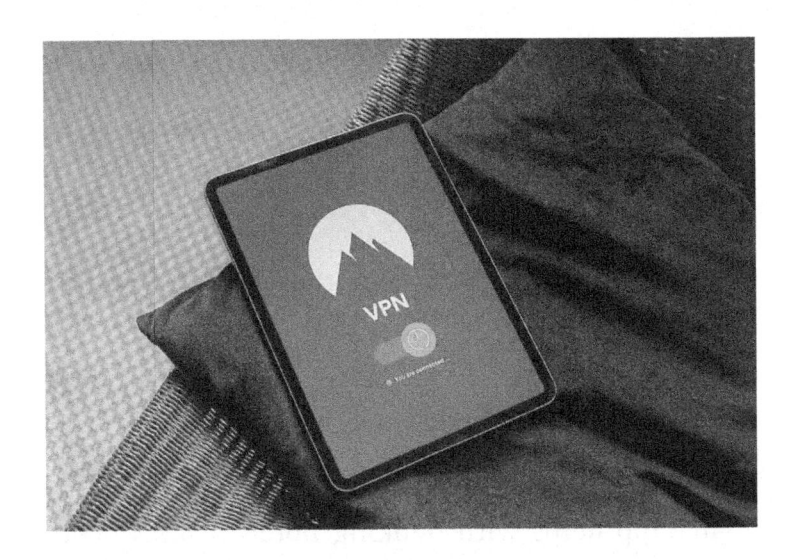

7. VPN App

Since many Western websites and apps, including Google, Facebook, and WhatsApp, are restricted in China, it's recommended to install a **VPN (Virtual**

Private Network) before arriving in the country. Popular options include ExpressVPN, NordVPN, and Surfshark.

Visiting the Great Wall of China is an unforgettable experience, but careful planning can make your trip even more rewarding. By avoiding common tourist mistakes, learning essential Mandarin phrases, and utilizing the right travel apps, you can navigate the Wall with confidence and ease. Whether you are exploring the bustling Badaling section or hiking the remote wild walls of Jiankou, being well-prepared ensures a smooth and enjoyable adventure.

CONCLUSION

As you embark on your journey, remember to **respect the historical site, support local communities, and practice responsible tourism**. The Great Wall is not just a relic of the past—it is a living testament to history, resilience, and cultural heritage. Travel smart, embrace the adventure, and create lasting memories of one of the world's greatest wonders.

The Great Wall of China is more than just an architectural marvel; it is a living testament to human perseverance, ingenuity, and the rich history of one of the world's oldest civilizations. Stretching across thousands of miles, winding through mountains, deserts, and valleys, the Wall has stood for centuries as a symbol of strength, protection, and unity. Whether you are drawn by its historical significance, breathtaking landscapes, or adventurous hikes, experiencing the Great Wall is a journey that will leave an indelible mark on your heart.

Visiting the Great Wall is not just about seeing an ancient structure—it is about **feeling the history beneath your feet**, imagining the stories of soldiers and builders who once stood guard, and embracing the cultural richness that surrounds it. Walking along the Wall, you will witness the contrast between restored sections with their imposing watchtowers and the rugged, untamed beauty of the wild walls, where nature has slowly reclaimed its place. Every step along the Wall tells a different story, offering a deep sense of connection to the past.

For history lovers, the Great Wall provides a window into the military strategies, engineering brilliance, and dynastic power struggles that shaped China. For adventure seekers, the Wall presents thrilling hikes, steep climbs, and the opportunity to push physical limits. For photographers, the Wall offers some of the most **spectacular sunrises, sunsets, and panoramic views** in the world. No matter your interest, the Great Wall of China has something to offer.

A well-prepared journey to the Great Wall ensures that you can fully immerse yourself in its grandeur without unnecessary stress. From choosing the right section to visit—whether it's the popular Badaling, the scenic Mutianyu, the adventurous Jiankou, or the remote Simatai—to **understanding local customs, packing appropriately, and using the right travel tools**, planning ahead makes all the difference.

Equipped with **useful Mandarin phrases**, an understanding of **local regulations**, and **essential travel apps**, you can navigate the Wall and its surroundings with ease. Whether you choose to hike, take a cable car, ride a toboggan, or even experience an aerial view from a **hot air balloon**, the Great Wall offers countless ways to explore its beauty.

As one of the world's most visited landmarks, the Great Wall faces significant challenges, including erosion, pollution, and damage from unregulated tourism. **As travelers, we have a duty to respect and preserve this UNESCO World Heritage Site** for future generations. Simple actions like **not littering, following designated trails, and respecting local guidelines** contribute to the Wall's longevity. Supporting local businesses, staying in sustainable accommodations, and participating in ethical tourism practices ensure that the communities surrounding the Wall also benefit from tourism.

Whether this is your first visit or a return trip, the Great Wall of China offers an experience that never fades. Standing atop its ancient stones, gazing out at the seemingly endless stretch of Wall disappearing into the horizon, you will feel a sense of wonder that few places on Earth can evoke. It is a reminder of the brilliance of past civilizations, the power of human endurance, and the timeless beauty of the natural world.

As you embark on your journey, take a moment to pause, breathe in the crisp mountain air, and reflect on the centuries of history surrounding you. The Great Wall is not just a destination—it is an adventure, a lesson in resilience, and a story waiting to be discovered. Travel wisely, embrace the experience, and let the Great Wall leave you with memories that will last a lifetime.

Made in the USA
Las Vegas, NV
17 May 2025